Geologic interpretation of magnetic and gravity data in the Copper River Basin, Alaska: USGS Professional Paper 316-H

et al., G. E. Andreasoen, Arthur Grantz

The BiblioGov Project is an effort to expand awareness of the public documents and records of the U.S. Government via print publications. In broadening the public understanding of government and its work, an enlightened democracy can grow and prosper. Ranging from historic Congressional Bills to the most recent Budget of the United States Government, the BiblioGov Project spans a wealth of government information. These works are now made available through an environmentally friendly, print-on-demand basis, using only what is necessary to meet the required demands of an interested public. We invite you to learn of the records of the U.S. Government, heightening the knowledge and debate that can lead from such publications.

Included are the following Collections:

Budget of The United States Government
Presidential Documents
United States Code
Education Reports from ERIC
GAO Reports
History of Bills
House Rules and Manual
Public and Private Laws

Code of Federal Regulations
Congressional Documents
Economic Indicators
Federal Register
Government Manuals
House Journal
Privacy act Issuances
Statutes at Large

Geologic Interpretation of Magnetic and Gravity Data in the Copper River Basin, Alaska

By GORDON E. ANDREASEN, ARTHUR GRANTZ, ISIDORE ZIETZ, *and* DAVID F. BARNES

GEOPHYSICAL FIELD INVESTIGATIONS

GEOLOGICAL SURVEY PROFESSIONAL PAPER 316-H

UNITED STATES GOVERNMENT PRINTING OFFICE, WASHINGTON : 1964

UNITED STATES DEPARTMENT OF THE INTERIOR

STEWART L. UDALL, *Secretary*

GEOLOGICAL SURVEY

Thomas B. Nolan, *Director*

The U.S. Geological Survey Library has cataloged this publication as follows:

Andreasen, Gordon Ellsworth, 1924–
    Geologic interpretation of magnetic and gravity data in
the Copper River Basin, Alaska, by Gordon E. Andreasen
[and others].   Washington, U.S. Govt. Print. Off., 1964.

    135–153 p.   maps (2 fold. col. in pocket) profiles, table.   30 cm.
(U.S. Geological Survey.   Professional paper 316–H)
    Geophysical field investigations.
    Bibliography: p. 152–153.

    1. Magnetism, Terrestrial—Alaska—Copper River Basin.   2. Geol-
ogy—Alaska—Copper River Basin.   I. Title.   (Series)

CONTENTS

ILLUSTRATIONS

[Plates are in pocket]

TABLE

III

GEOLOGIC INTERPRETATION OF MAGNETIC AND GRAVITY DATA IN THE COPPER RIVER BASIN, ALASKA

By Gordon E. Andreasen, Arthur Grantz,
Isidore Zietz, and David F. Barnes

ABSTRACT

Aeromagnetic and gravity surveys were made of approximately 6,500 square miles of the Copper River Basin, Alaska.

Magnetic data, compiled as a total-intensity contour map, show patterns that closely parallel the generally arcuate geologic "grain" and seemingly can be correlated with lithology and geologic structure. Areas where volcanic rocks crop out are indicated by a characteristic configuration of magnetic contours. The magnetic data suggest that Lower Jurassic volcanic rocks exposed in the Talkeetna and northern Chugach Mountains underlie sedimentary rocks in the southwest quadrant of the surveyed area. The data also indicate that Tertiary and Quaternary lavas of the Wrangell Mountains occur at shallow depths in the eastern part of the Copper River Basin in the vicinity of Mount Drum. Alternate bands of high and low magnetic values characterize much of the northern third of the surveyed area and are interpreted as products of the plutonic rocks and metamorphosed volcanic and sedimentary rocks that crop out at many places.

Large negative Bouguer gravity anomalies were observed in two areas where the magnetic gradients are low and where the sedimentary rocks may be thick. One of these areas is near Old Man Lake in the southwestern part of the surveyed area, and there the lowest gravity values were measured; the other area occupies most of the southeast quadrant of the Copper River Basin, where the gravity values decrease toward the Wrangell Mountains. The largest Bouguer anomalies are associated with outcrops of lower Mesozoic volcanic rocks and Paleozoic basement rocks north and south of these gravity lows. The 60-milligal difference between the low- and high-gravity values probably represents, at least in part, an increased thickness of post-Lower Jurassic sedimentary rocks.

INTRODUCTION

An aeromagnetic survey of the Copper River Basin was made by the U.S. Geological Survey in 1954 and 1955, and more than 700 gravity stations were obtained in approximately the same area between 1958 and 1960. Both surveys supported geologic field mapping projects in and adjacent to the Copper River Basin and were planned so that the geophysical data would assist the geologic mapping and the interpretation of the subsurface geology.

AREA COVERED

The Copper River Basin is a broad topographic depression bounded by the Alaska Range on the north, the Wrangell Mountains on the east, the Chugach Mountains on the south, and the Talkeetna Mountains on the west (fig. 47). Wahrhaftig (1960) divided the Basin into two physiographic subdivisions—the Lake Louise Plateau on the west, entirely included within the surveyed area, and Copper River Valley on the east, most of which is included in the surveyed area. The north side of the surveyed area also includes almost all of another physiographic division, the Gulkana Upland, which comprises the southern foothills of the Alaska Range. Fringes of four other physiographic divisions, the Talkeetna Mountains, the Matanuska Valley, the Kenai-Chugach Mountains, and the Wrangell Mountains, complete the area covered by the survey.

AEROMAGNETIC SURVEY

The aeromagnetic survey covered approximately 6,500 square miles and consisted of 75 north-south traverses approximately 80 miles long and spaced 1 mile apart. The flight lines extend north from the northern Chugach Mountains to lat 63°00′ N. in the southern foothills of the Alaska Range. The easternmost line, at long 145°00′ W., skirts the 2,600-foot contour of the western Wrangell Mountains; the westernmost line, at long 147°20′ W., crosses the eastern foothills of the Talkeetna Mountains.

Aeromagnetic traverses were flown at a barometric flight elevation of 4,000 feet, except locally where topography required higher flight elevations. Continuous total-intensity magnetic data along flight traverses were obtained from a modified AN/ASQ-3A airborne magnetometer from which a fluxgate-type detecting element was towed about 75 feet below the aircraft. Flight lines plotted on topographic maps at a scale of 1:63,360 were used for flight guidance. The actual

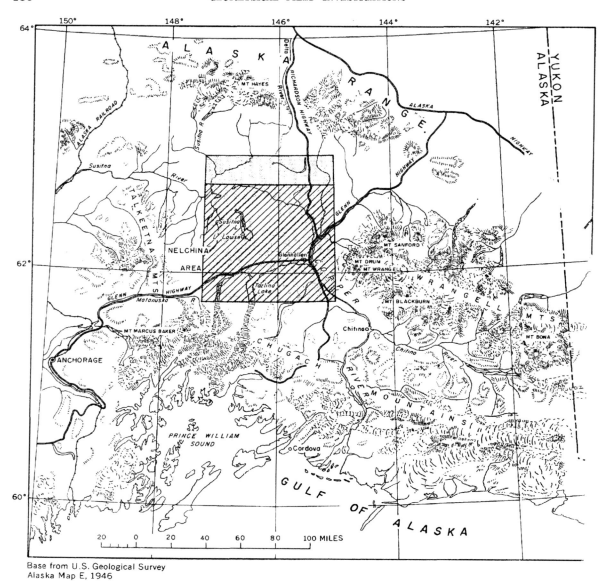

Base from U.S. Geological Survey
Alaska Map E, 1946

FIGURE 47.—Index map showing location of the Copper River Basin area. Area of aeromagnetic survey stippled; area of gravity survey diagonally ruled.

flight paths were recorded by a gyro-stabilized continuous-strip camera. These data were compiled and published as a total-intensity magnetic-contour map (Andreasen and others, 1958). This map is essentially the same as the one presented in this report as plate 23. The aeromagnetic-contour map has not been corrected for the earth's normal magnetic gradient. According to Vestine and others (1947), the earth's normal total magnetic-field intensity in the Copper River region increases approximately 5 gammas per mile in a northeasterly direction.

GRAVITY SURVEY

Gravity data were obtained throughout the area of the aeromagnetic survey, but the Bouguer contour map does not cover the northern fifth of the aeromagnetic-survey area where the station density was too low to permit contouring. The data were obtained with a Worden gravimeter having a scale constant of 0.242 mgal (milligal) per scale division. Observed gravity values were based on a measurement of 981.9309 gals made at Gulkana Airport by Thiel and others (1958). Simple Bouguer corrections using a density of 2.67 g per cm³ (grams per cubic centimeter) were made for all stations, and terrain corrections to Hayford's zone M were made for more than 75 stations and estimated for the remaining stations. Computed terrain corrections range from 8 mgal on the mountainous fringes of the basin to less than 0.2 mgal in the marshy, central part of the basin. The Bouguer anomalies were compiled as a contour map having a 5-mgal contour interval. The measurements should be accurate to within one-tenth of the contour interval except at a few stations where altimeter elevations were used and where errors may amount to half a contour interval.

ACKNOWLEDGMENTS

Many members of the U.S. Geological Survey participated in the preparation of this report and its accompanying maps. J. R. Henderson was in charge of the flying in 1954, and G. E. Andreasen completed the survey in 1955. W. T. Kinoshita, C. R. Willden, H. F. Bennett, R. V. Allen, and D. F. Barnes collected various parts of the gravity data, and R. C. Jachens assisted in its reduction and interpretation. The geologic description of the Copper River Basin area and the accompanying geologic map (pl. 24) were prepared primarily from the reference listed in the explanation of plate 23. However, the geologic data include a few field observations by F. R. Collins, F. R. Weber, J. R. Williams, D. R. Nichols, D. L. Rossman, and Arthur Grantz.

GEOLOGY

The Copper River Basin is a structural and topographic basin drained chiefly by the Copper River and, secondarily, by the Susitna, Matanuska, and Delta Rivers.

Quaternary glacial and alluvial deposits and local continental deposits of Eocene age are present over most of the basin and conceal the older rocks (pl. 23). Pre-Eocene rocks in general form eastward-trending arcs that are concave south (see Payne, 1955). These arcs existed in Mesozoic and earliest Tertiary time and are delineated by the strike of geologic contacts, faults, and topographic features. Among the arcuate features are two belts of lower Jurassic and older rocks that contain numerous plutonic intrusive rocks and are called the Seldovia and Talkeetna geanticlines. These geanticlines trend eastward through the northern part of the Chugach Mountains and the northern half of the Copper River Basin, respectively. Between the geanticlines lies a belt of marine sedimentary rocks of Middle Jurassic through Late Cretaceous age that was deposited in the Matanuska geosyncline. These rocks trend into the basin from the Matanuska Valley on the west and from the Chitina Valley on the southeast, but they are exposed at only a few places within the basin.

ROCK UNITS

CARBONIFEROUS AND OLDER ROCKS

A variety of metamorphosed sedimentary and volcanic rocks of Carboniferous and possibly older(?) age crop out in and adjacent to the Copper River Basin. These rocks are of very low to intermediate metamorphic grade. Their lithology, age, and correlation have been determined at only a few places; and for the purpose of this report, they are grouped into two map units.

One unit includes (1) metamorphosed volcanic and sedimentary rocks, which occur in the Talkeetna geanticline and crop out in a low range of eastward-trending hills in the northern part of the basin; (2) the Tetelna Volcanics, which crop out east of the Chistochina River; and (3) the Dadina Schist and Strelna Formation, which crop out between Mount Drum and the lower Chitina River. Andesitic and basaltic lavas and tuffs that in most places have been altered to greenstone and greenschist predominate, but the unit contains slate, quartzite and quartzose schist, phyllite, biotite schist, limestone, schistose amphibolite, shale, and chert. Chlorite and magnetite are abundant in the metavolcanic rocks. Diorite, quartz diorite, and mafic intrusives, in many places altered, have been recognized in this unit, but most have not been mapped. In the Chitina Valley the Strelna Formation of unit Cvs is more than 6,500 feet thick.

The second map unit of Carboniferous and older(?) rocks consists mostly of metamorphosed sedimentary rocks. It occurs in the southeastern and northeastern parts of the Copper River Basin; contains argillite, quartzite, conglomerate, siliceous sediments, limestone, quartz, mica schist, and some tuff and lava flows; and includes the Klutina Group and the Chisna Formation. Plutons of diverse lithologies have intruded these rocks, and, undoubtedly, many more occur than have been mapped.

PERMIAN AND TRIASSIC ROCKS

Altered basalt and andesite flows containing intercalated tuffaceous and shaly beds of Permian and Triassic(?) ages crop out in a broad band across the northern part of the Copper River Basin and in the Chitina Valley, where they are known as the Nikolai Greenstone. They are more than 5,000 feet thick in the northern part of the surveyed area and perhaps 6,500 feet or' more thick in the Chitina Valley. About 5,000 feet of Late Triassic sedimentary rocks (Trs) (the Chitistone and Nizina Limestones and the McCarthy Shale and the Kuskulana Formation) overlie the Nikolai Greenstone in the Chitina Valley.

JURASSIC VOLCANIC AND ASSOCIATED ROCKS

Altered marine pyroclastic rocks—in general andesitic but ranging from rhyolite to basalt—lava flows, and tuffaceous sedimentary rocks occur in the Talkeetna Mountains and in the northern Chugach Mountains west of Tazlina Lake; the upper beds of the sequence are predominantly sedimentary. These rocks are part of the Talkeetna Formation of Early Jurassic age and are at least several thousand feet thick. Lower Jurassic volcanic rocks are not present in the Chitina Valley and have not been reported from the eastern and northern parts of the Copper River Basin. However, marine sedimentary rocks of Early Jurassic age occur in the upper Chitina Valley (E. M. MacKevett, oral communication, 1962), and possibly occur in map units Trs or KJs in the lower Chitina Valley. Thus, the southeastern part of the Basin may be underlain by Lower Jurassic rocks of a facies transitional between the lava-bearing Talkeetna Formation and the sedimentary rocks of the upper Chitina Valley.

Volcanic rocks in the northern Chugach Mountains between Tazlina Lake and Stuck Mountain have been referred to the Lower Jurassic (Talkeetna Formation) by Chapin (1918, pl. 2) and to the Carboniferous by Moffit (1938a, pl. 2). These strata are shown as volcanic rocks of Carboniferous or Jurassic age on plate 23, because rocks of both systems may be included in this map unit.

JURASSIC AND CRETACEOUS SEDIMENTARY ROCKS

A unit of marine sedimentary rocks deposited in the Matanuska geocyncline rests unconformably upon the Talkeetna Formation in the southwestern part of the Copper River Basin and on Early Jurassic or Late Triassic and older rocks in the Chitina Valley. These rocks do not crop out anywhere else in the Copper River Basin, and were probably not deposited in its northern part. In the southwestern part of Copper River Basin they consist of siltstone, shale, sandstone, conglomerate, and limestone of the Tuxedni, Chinitna, and Naknek Formations of Jurassic age, the Nelchina Limestone and associated beds of Early Cretaceous age, and the Matanuska Formation of late Early and Late Cretaceous age. The Jurassic and Lower Cretaceous beds total about 7,500 feet in thickness and occur chiefly north of

the Matanuska Formation, which may total 10,000 f in thickness. The Kennicott Formation, Kotsina Co glomerate, and several unnamed units in the Chiti Valley are included in the marine sedimentary roc and in places are thousands of feet thick.

INTRUSIVE ROCKS

Igneous masses ranging in size from dikes to batl liths occur mainly in the rocks of the Seldovia and T keetna geanticlines. Except for those igneous mas associated with the Wrangell Lava, the igneous roc range in age from late Paleozoic to latest Cretaceous possibly Paleocene. Quartz diorite is most comm but granodiorite, granite, gabbro, and ultramafic roc occur also. Some of the intrusive rocks have be metamorphosed. Only the largest intrusions have be mapped, and these only locally. The intrusives show on plate 23 are but a small part of those in the area.

TERTIARY SEDIMENTARY ROCKS

Continental sediments of Eocene age [1] were deposit on an extensive surface of low relief that was formed Eocene time. These sediments are now represented sandstone, conglomerate, siltstone, claystone, and, cally, beds of coal. Eocene plants have been collect from the strata at a few places. Several hundred fe of these rocks are present in the southwestern part the basin, but complete sections have not been four These Tertiary sedimentary rocks may be much thick where buried by Quaternary deposits, especially in t area north of the latitude of Glennallen. The Eoce sedimentary rocks are more than 2,000 feet thick in t northern part of the basin, where they have been nam the Gakona Formation.

CENOZOIC VOLCANIC ROCKS

The Wrangell Lava makes up the bulk of the Wra gell Mountains. It includes lavas of Eocene [2] a Quaternary age and in places is interbedded with Ple tocene glacial deposits. It consists chiefly of andes lava flows and associated pyroclastic rocks but contai some basalt and dacite. Basalt flows and min amounts of more felsic rocks and pyroclastic rocks cr out extensively in the southeast Talkeetna Mountai Eocene [2] plants have been collected from the pyroclas rocks.

Glacial and alluvial deposits of Quaternary age ma older rocks in most of the Copper River Basin. The deposits are more than 600 feet thick at places and m exceed 1,000 feet in thickness.

[1] Recent paleontological studies by Jack A. Wolfe of the Geolog Survey indicate that these deposits and the erosion surface upon wh they rest are of Oligocene age.
[2] See footnote 1.

PHYSICAL-PROPERTY MEASUREMENTS

The geophysical expression of these rock units depends on their physical properties, and measurements of hand-specimen densities and magnetic properties were performed as part of the geophysical study. Most specimens used for these measurements were obtained from easily accessible outcrops or in the course of geologic-mapping programs. The results satisfactorily show the relative geophysical effects of the principal rock units. However, not all mapped units were sampled, and the distribution of samples may not provide a statistical sampling of each formation. Furthermore, the physical properties of some specimens may have been altered by weathering.

Densities were measured by comparing weights in water and in air. Many density measurements were made after the specimens had been dried overnight in a vacuum and then soaked in water, so that water-saturated rocks were represented by the averages. The results of the density measurements are shown in table 1.

TABLE 1.—*Densities of Copper River Basin rock units, in grams per cubic centimeter*

Rock group	Number of specimens	Density		
		Minimum	Maximum	Average
Carboniferous and older	16	2.61	3.04	2.85
Permian and Triassic	2	2.93	2.98	[1] 2.96
Jurassic and older volcanic rocks	38	2.29	2.88	2.64
Jurassic and Cretaceous sedimentary rocks	51	2.29	2.93	2.58
Intrusive rocks	15	2.38	2.76	2.61
Tertiary sedimentary rocks	11	1.90	2.56	2.30
Cenozoic volcanic rocks	2	2.66	2.69	[1] 2.67

[1] Average based on only two specimens.

The densest rocks found in the surveyed area are the metamorphosed Paleozoic volcanic and associated sedimentary rocks. (No samples of the Paleozoic sedimentary formations were measured, but these rocks may be less dense.) The overlying Mesozoic volcanic and sedimentary rocks are less dense, but their density varies considerably with changes in geographic and stratigraphic position. Thus, the densities of 51 specimens of Matanuska sedimentary rocks average 2.58 g per cm³, whereas the average for specimens found near the center of the basin is lower; several specimens of Matanuska siltstone from a drill hole near Eureka have an average density of 2.53. The least dense rocks in the area are in general the Tertiary sedimentary rocks, but the density of the overlying layer of Quaternary outwash and glacial deposits is probably even lower. Only two specimens of the Cenozoic lavas that make up the Wrangell Mountains were measured, so the density of this formation may be much different from the average of 2.67 g per cm³ indicated by the two specimens.

Magnetic properties of hand specimens from the Copper River Basin were examined qualitatively by placing them in the field of a Schmidt vertical magnetometer according to a modification of the method of Hyslop (1945). The induced magnetization exceeded the remanent magnetization of all except a few specimens of Jurassic and Carboniferous volcanic rocks and of Middle Jurassic sandstone containing local concentrations of magnetite. Strong remanent magnetism is present in more parts of the Talkeetna Formation than in any other rock in the surveyed area, and magnetic-susceptibility measurements for this formation also showed a wide range (from less than 0.001 to more than 0.01 cgs unit). However, high values and a wide range of magnetic susceptibility are also found in many specimens of Paleozoic volcanic rocks, intrusive rocks, and Tertiary volcanic rocks. Almost all specimens of Jurassic and Cretaceous marine and Teritary continental sedimentary rocks have susceptibilities below 0.005, and values below 0.001 predominate.

STRUCTURE

The arcuate easterly trend of most geologic features across south-central Alaska is well formed in the Copper River Basin, and the north face of the Chugach Mountains marks a structural front that follows this trend. The strike of the Mesozoic marine rocks and their basal contacts in the Nelchina area and Chitina Valley, the alined bedrock hills in the northern Copper River Basin, and the trends of the Carboniferous and older(?) volcanic and sedimentary rocks and the belt of Permian and Triassic volcanic rocks in the northern part of the basin also reflect the regional trend.

East- and northeast-striking faults, fault blocks, and folds dominate the structure of the Nelchina area. The probable extension of the Castle Mountain reverse fault, which lies on the north side of the Matanuska Valley, trends eastward across the Nelchina area to the Copper River Basin, but much of its displacement is dissipated in northeast-striking branch faults in the Nelchina area. Eocene sedimentary rocks and Cenozoic lavas in general dip gently, but locally they dip steeply and are faulted.

Unconformities within the Jurassic, Cretaceous, and Tertiary rocks, and the erosion they represent, have had an important influence on the present distribution of the Jurassic and younger sedimentary formations. Marine sedimentary rocks of Mesozoic age were deposited as a series of overlapping prisms, and all do not occur in any one vertical section. The Eocene sedimentary rocks were deposited in basins and on pediments whose distribution is unrelated to the patterns of Mesozoic deposition.

MAGNETIC AND GRAVITY INTERPRETATION
TECHNIQUES

The aeromagnetic data have been compiled as a total-intensity contour map (pl. 23), and the gravity data are presented as a Bouguer-anomaly contour map (pl. 24). Both maps show geophysical features that can be correlated by geologic mapping along the margins of the basin, where there are sufficient outcrops to permit the determination of geologic structure. A large part of the interpretation of the Copper River aeromagnetic data involves the comparison of magnetic patterns over anomaly-producing rocks of known lithology with the patterns observed in areas where similar anomaly-producing rocks are masked by a cover of essentially nonmagnetic sedimentary rocks. Both the gravity and magnetic data provide, in a few places, estimates of the thickness of these overlying sedimentary rocks.

The methods of magnetic depth interpretation used in this report are essentially the same as those described by Vacquier and others (1951). Briefly, the assumptions upon which the magnetic interpretation is based are:

1. Anomalies of large amplitude and wide areal extent are produced by contrasts in magnetic susceptibility (topographic relief of a magnetic rock unit generally produces only small amplitude anomalies).
2. Anomaly-producing rocks are magnetically homogeneous and are magnetized in the earth's field.
3. Remanent magnetization is in the direction of the earth's field or is negligible.
4. Rock masses producing anomalies possess a plane surface and vertical sides and are of infinite depth extent.

A magnetic rock mass whose thickness is equal to or greater than the height of the magnetometer above the upper surface of the mass seems, magnetically, to be of infinite depth extent. If remanent magnetization is great and of nonrandom orientation, or if the magnetic mass is too thin to meet the infinite-depth-extent requirement, the method is not applicable. Depth estimates based on the magnetic field produced by a thin sheet of magnetic mass are too shallow. In this report, depth estimates are based on the assumption of infinite depth extent.

For the few anomalies suitable to quantitative analysis by this method, the estimation of depths to the upper surface of the magnetic rock units involves the comparison of observed profiles with suitable computed profiles for rectangular prismatic models. An approximation of depths of burial can be obtained by measuring the horizontal extent of the steepest gradient of the anomaly, taken at right angles to the contours.

REGIONAL MAGNETIC PATTERNS AND GRAVITY ANOMALIES

The principal magnetic patterns of the Copper River Basin are shown on a simplified aeromagnetic map (fig. 48), contoured at intervals of 200, 400, or 600 gammas. Areas where the magnetic intensity is less than 4,500 gammas (arbitrarily chosen) are shaded so that the several distinct magnetic patterns are more clearly apparent. Figure 4 shows that the general trend of the total magnetic intensity is parallel to the arcuate geologic grain of the area. Examples are the east-trending magnetic highs over the northern Chugach Mountains and the east-trending belts of magnetic highs and lows—called in this report the Maclaren-Gulkana anomalies—across most of the northern third of the Copper River Basin. Perhaps the most conspicuous magnetic anomaly—called in this report the West Fork feature— traverses the area at approximately lat 62°35′ N. This feature is bounded on the north by a steep magnetic gradient that is continuous for at least 75 miles and is several hundred gammas in amplitude. The Tyone Creek anomalies in the west-central part of the Copper River Basin constitute another distinct magnetic pattern. Here, numerous steep-gradient anomalies have amplitudes ranging from about 200 to 700 gammas. Another distinct magnetic pattern—called in this report the Mount Drum pattern—occurs at the east edge of the area from about lat 62°00′ to 62°25′ N. A discussion of these and several other magnetic features (shown in fig. 48) follows shortly.

The most conspicuous anomaly shown on the gravity map is the broad low centered around Old Man Lake in the west-central part of the map. This low is bordered on the north and south by gravity highs that include Bouguer anomalies above −25 mgal. North and south of these gravity highs the gravity decreases to low values which have been measured in the central parts of the Alaska Range and Chugach Mountains. East and west of the Old Man Lake gravity low the Bouguer anomalies are not as high as those on its north and south sides; Bouguer anomalies of −50 to −60 mgal separate the Old Man Lake low from other low values measured in the Wrangell and Talkeetna Mountains outside the mapped area. Gravity lows and highs are thus arranged in east-trending belts that cross the mapped area and approximately parallel the arcuate pattern of the geologic structure and magnetic anomalies. The mapped area does not include the central parts of the adjoining mountain ranges, where only a few gravity measurements have been made. The regional gradient in the Copper River Basin is, therefore, best determined by comparing the gravity observations in the high areas bordering the Old Man Lake low. Bouguer anomalies on the northern high, in the foothills of the Alaska Range, are about 10 mgal lower than those in the southern high, along the edge of the Chugach Mountains. A similar comparison of the gravity values on the east and west sides of the low shows a gravity decrease toward the east. These two comparisons indicate a regional gradient of decreasing gravity toward the northeast, or toward the interior of the continent. Such gravity decreases that extend over long distances probably represent increasing thickness of the continental crust.

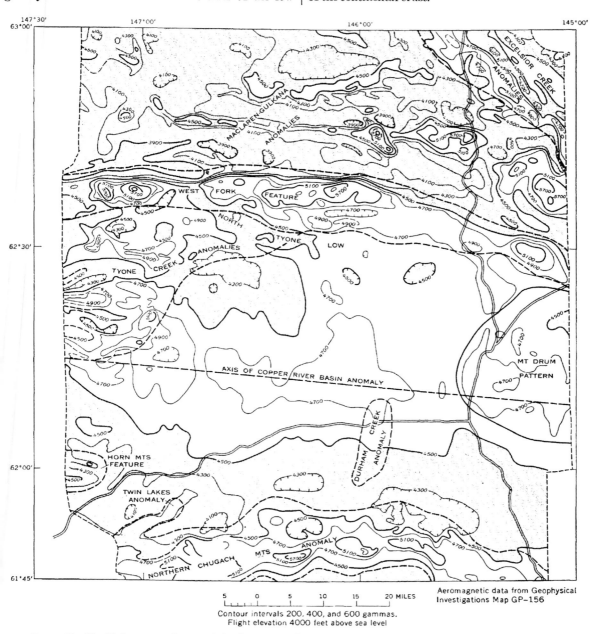

FIGURE 48.—Simplified aeromagnetic map of the Copper River Basin area, Alaska. Areas of less than 4,500 gammas are shaded.

ANOMALIES IN THE NORTHERN PART OF THE SURVEYED AREA

EXCELSIOR CREEK ANOMALIES

In the extreme northeast corner of the surveyed area, belts of essentially linear magnetic highs and lows (pl. 23; fig. 48) trend southeast and form the Excelsior Creek anomalies. Individual anomalies range in amplitude from a few hundred gammas to about 1,200 gammas. The steep gradients characteristic of these anomalies indicate that the rock masses causing the disturbance are at or very near the ground surface. Most Excelsior Creek anomalies are north of the area covered by the detailed gravity survey, but a very few contours at the extreme northeast corner of the gravity map seem to parallel the southeast trend of the magnetic contours.

Excelsior Creek anomalies are believed to be produced by southeast-trending belts of rocks that include the Permian and Triassic(?) basalt and andesite (pl. 23), as these volcanic rocks have been mapped over part of the southwesternmost of the two regional magnetic highs. The Excelsior Creek anomalies cut across the magnetic and geologic trend that is dominant to the west; hence, the southwest margin of the anomalies probably marks a structural discontinuity.

MACLAREN-GULKANA ANOMALIES

Metamorphosed volcanic and sedimentary rocks of Carboniferous and older(?) age have been mapped in the alined isolated hills that trend eastward across the northern third of the surveyed area in the region of the Maclaren and Gulkana Rivers. Magnetically, this area is characterized by east-trending belts of steep-gradient magnetic highs and lows ranging in amplitude from a few hundred gammas to more than 2,000 gammas. The east-west magnetic lineations reflect the trends of the rock masses producing the anomalies, as in the instance of the Excelsior Creek anomalies. The bands of magnetic highs may be produced by igneous rock, and the bands of magnetic lows, by sedimentary rocks. Such alternate bands of igneous and sedimentary rocks could provide the appreciable and abrupt change in magnetic susceptibility or magnetite content necessary to produce the observed magnetic anomalies. It is unlikely that topographic relief on the upper surface of the magnetic rock mass alone could account for the amplitudes of the observed magnetic anomalies in this area, through it may have increased them somewhat. The steep gradients characteristic of most Maclaren-Gulkana anomalies suggest that the magnetic rock masses are at or near the ground surface.

Gravity profiles along the Richardson Highway and the Maclaren River crossed the area covered by the Maclaren-Gulkana gravity anomalies and showed that these anomalies are large and closely spaced. Except for stations along those profiles, however, the gravity stations in this northern part of the mapped area are widely spaced, and contouring is uncertain and is indicated by dashed lines on plate 24. However, some correlation can be observed between the major gravity and magnetic features. The −77-mgal gravity low north of the abandoned Haggard Road Camp and the −67 mgal low north of the bend in the Tyone River (pl. 24) approximately coincide with areas occupied by magnetic highs. A third area containing Bouguer anomalies as low as −104 mgal and coinciding with magnetic lows was observed north of the mapped area and downstream from the Maclaren River rapids.

At present, the lack of detailed geologic information in the Maclaren-Gulkana area precludes any attempt to correlate geophysical patterns with rock types. For example, the densities and magnetic effects of the numerous, but unmapped, igneous intrusive rocks of many types known to crop out in this area are uncertain. A variety of gneissic granitic rocks have been observed on the high ridge that coincides with the elongate magnetic high and −67-mgal gravity low north of the Tyrone River bend. However, three other areas where intrusions have been mapped seem to correlate with magnetic lows. The pronounced magnetic trend should aid geologic mapping in this area, where bedrock is in most places hidden by surficial deposits.

WEST FORK FEATURE

A remarkably linear group of closely spaced contours marks the north side of a magnetic high that crosses the entire surveyed area at about lat 62°35′ N. This magnetic high, called the West Fork feature, is essentially one anomaly with several superimposed magnetic highs and lows. Its trend closely follows the West Fork of the Gulkana River, and its overall length exceeds the 75-mile width of the mapped area. A pronounced magnetic gradient on the north side of the feature indicates a significant and abrupt change in lithology. The gradient may be produced by a fault or steeply dipping contact separating a linear rock body of high susceptibility on the south from rocks of lower susceptibility on the north. The south slope of the feature is less distinct, and in the western part of the area the south slope is nearly obscured by many superimposed steep-gradient magnetic highs and lows that are probably produced by near-surface volcanic or intrusive rocks. In this western area the width of the West Fork feature is uncertain, but throughout the eastern two thirds of the magnetic map area the width ranges between 3 and 10 miles and averages about 6 miles.

High gravity values are also associated with the West Fork feature, but the gravity map does not indicate the linear continuity suggested by the aeromagnetic map. Three gravity highs of different form and magnitude are near the axis of the magnetic feature and probably are caused by the same rock unit. The West Fork gravity feature can thus be divided into three units that can be described separately.

The linearity of the feature is best shown in the central part of the mapped area between long 145°50′ and 146°40′ W. Here, it is represented by an elongate gravity high for which the Bouguer anomalies range as high as −22 mgal and by a similarly shaped group of magnetic highs that range as high as 6,300 gammas. The gravity and magnetic gradients on the south side of the feature are well defined, although they are not as steep as those on the north side; the widths of both the gravity and the magnetic highs are approximately 7 miles. Estimates of depth to the upper surface of the disturbing mass can be calculated from the magnetic gradient on the north side of the feature; these estimates range from 700 to 1,000 feet below land surface in this central part of the mapped area. The less steep gradients on the south side of the West Fork feature suggest that the disturbing rock mass may dip southward, although other explanations are also possible.

The West Fork feature changes in character along a northeast-trending magnetic contact near Fish Lake at long 145°50′ W. Here, the numerous steep-gradient magnetic highs that characterize the western part of the feature are subdued or absent east of this magnetic contact, and the gravity high is either absent or displaced to the north. Depths to the mass producing the anomaly are estimated from the magnetic gradient as 700 to 1,000 feet in the central part of the feature increasing to 1,500 feet near Fish Lake and to 1,800 where the Gulkana River crosses the feature. The top of the mass producing the magnetic feature is at greater depths to the east, and about 2 miles east of the Richardson Highway it is about 3,000 feet below the ground surface. Estimates of depth to the magnetic feature near the east margin of the surveyed area are 4,000 to 5,000 feet. This increasing depth to the feature suggests a cover of sediments or sedimentary rocks that thickens southeast of Fish Lake. The gravity anomaly produced by such a sedimentary prism would mask or reduce the gravity anomaly produced by the West Fork rock mass and, if the sedimentary prism thickened southward, would tend to shift the gravity maximum northward. Possibly the gravity maximum found along the Richardson Highway approximately half way between the axis of the West Fork magnetic feature and the southernmost outcrop of basement rocks at

Hogan Hill is the gravity anomaly of the West Fork rock mass that has been shifted northward in this manner. This gravity high extends southeastward and is parallel to the West Fork magnetic feature. A cover of light sediments or sedimentary rocks that thins could thus account for both the deepening of the West Fork magnetic feature and the coincident displacement of the gravity anomaly to the north of the magnetic feature in the area east of Fish Lake.

The west end of the West Fork feature is less clearly defined than the central and eastern parts, and it is separated from the central part by a belt of low gravity and magnetic values called in this report the North Tyone low. A broad gravity high and many steep-gradient magnetic anomalies cover a wide area southwest of the North Tyone low. The West Fork feature can be distinguished along the north side of this area by a line of very steep gradient magnetic highs and by the pronounced gradient along their north side. However, the south side of the feature is almost obscured by the poor contrast of geophysical anomalies between it and the rocks to the south. Measurements of depth to the source of the magnetic anomalies are almost the same for the western part of the West Fork feature as for its shallow central part. If the West Fork feature extends another 10 miles west of the edge of the magnetic map area, it trends into the dioritic rocks of the Talkeetna batholith in the Talkeetna Mountains.

The West Fork feature lies between mapped areas of metamorphosed Carboniferous rocks and possibly older volcanic and sedimentary rocks to the north and the partly altered volcanic rocks, tentatively correlated with the Lower Jurassic volcanic sequence that crop out north of Tyone Lake. Geologic mapping has not yet shown what type of rock formation has caused the feature nor the relation of the feature to adjacent rocks.

NORTH TYONE LOW

A row of magnetic and gravity lows intersects the West Fork feature along a line nearly parallel to, and north of, the Tyone River. The North Tyone low is best shown on the gravity map (pl. 24), where it is represented by a 15-mgal decrease in Bouguer anomaly. The magnetic lows (delineated by the dot-dash line on pl. 24) extend southeast from the steep gradient on the north side of the West Fork feature to Crosswind Lake or possibly beyond this lake as far as Ewan Lake. The trend of the low is oblique to the dominant structural grain of the Copper River Basin. The low-density rocks with low susceptibility or reversed remanent magnetization which cause the anomaly could be either intrusive or sedimentary rocks. Felsic intrusives and hornfels were found at the only bedrock outcrop that was investigated within the area covered by the North Tyone low, and these rocks probably do not cause the geophysical anomalies. The rocks causing the feature are presumably buried by sediments at the southeast end of the low.

ANOMALIES ON THE WEST AND SOUTH SIDES OF THE SURVEYED AREA

Magnetic anomalies along the west and south sides of the Copper River Basin are generally associated with Lower Jurassic volcanic rocks. The complex steep-gradient high-amplitude magnetic anomalies near Tyone Creek, the Horn Mountains, and the northern Chugach Mountains occur where the volcanic rocks are at or near the surface. Between these high-amplitude anomalies the volcanic rocks are buried by sedimentary rocks, and the magnetic pattern becomes more open, gradients less steep, and amplitudes of anomalies lower. The Lower Jurassic volcanic rocks are also inferred, on the basis of similar but subdued magnetic patterns, to be present beneath the sediments of the southern Copper River Basin as far east as the dot-dash line near long 146°15' W. (pl. 23).

Where the Lower Jurassic rocks are close to the surface, the Bouguer gravity anomalies are generally high; where they are buried by sediments, the anomalies are generally low. However, the values of Bouguer gravity anomalies vary considerably between different areas of outcrop of the Jurassic volcanic rocks and suggest that the gravity field is also influenced by the thickness of underlying Mesozoic and late Paleozoic rocks and by regional gravity gradients.

TYONE CREEK ANOMALIES

Steep-gradient high-amplitude magnetic anomalies occur over a broad area drained by Tyone Creek. The upper surface of the anomaly-producing rocks is calculated to be at or very near ground surface over most of the area west and north of the dashed line shown on plate 23. The rocks believed to produce most, if not all, of the Tyone Creek anomalies are the Lower Jurassic volcanic rocks (Talkeetna Formation) that crop out at several places along the southeast side of the area. Magnetic data show that these volcanic rocks extend at shallow depth under the area northwest of these outcrops where the surface material comprises alluvial or glacial deposits. The Tyone Creek anomalies and the linear magnetic highs associated with the West Fork feature are believed to be produced by rocks of a different lithology, but the boundary between the two is rather obscure. A dotted line on plate 23 approximately separates the Tyone Creek anomalies from the West Fork feature.

A broad gravity high covers most of the area occupied by the Tyone Creek anomalies. The highest gravity values occur north of the known volcanic rock outcrops and suggest that the pre-Mesozoic basement rocks may be closest to the surface in the central part of the area occupied by the Tyone Creek magnetic anomalies. Calculations based on the 0.2-g per cm³ density contract between the Talkeetna Formation and the underlying Paleozoic rocks and on the 12-mgal difference between the highest gravity values of the Tyone Creek anomalies and the lower gravity measured at outcrops of upper parts of the Talkeetna Formation suggest that the thickness of the Talkeetna in the central part of this area may be about 1 mile; this figure agrees with estimates obtained from geologic mapping.

HORN MOUNTAINS FEATURE

The Horn Mountains can be structurally generalized as a fault block of Lower Jurassic volcanic rocks in contact with sedimentary rocks to the north and to the south. The volcanic rocks produce two steep-gradient magnetic anomalies collectively called in this report the Horn Mountains feature. These anomalies extend eastward into the Copper River Basin approximately 5 miles beyond the easternmost outcrops of volcanic rocks. They are here terminated by closely spaced northeast-trending magnetic contours (pl. 23) that could possibly be produced by an extension of the fault bounding the Horn Mountains fault block on the south. Another magnetic gradient coincides with, and is interpreted to represent, the north-bounding fault of the Horn Mountains fault block. These magnetic contours continue east-southeastward from the last exposure of the fault and terminate at the northeast-trending contours. The faults bounding the Horn Mountains on the north and south sides and their extensions, as determined from the magnetic data, conform with the patterns of faulting observed in the Nelchina area.

The Horn Mountains fault block does not cause a significant gravity anomaly, although gravity contours diverge near the feature and indicate a decrease in the regional gradient. Values of Bouger anomaly associated with the feature are in the range of −40 to −50 mgal, or approximately the same as the values associated with the outcrops of Talkeetna volcanics in the southern part of the Tyone Creek area.

NORTHERN CHUGACH MOUNTAINS ANOMALIES

The steep-gradient east-trending intense magnetic anomalies found in the northern Chugach Mountains are virtually uniform in character across the surveyed area and are produced by magnetic rocks at or near the surface. These anomalies are attributed to Lower Jurassic lavas and tuffs which are known to crop out in the northern Chugach Mountains as far east as Tazlina Lake. Similar rocks, whose age has not been determined, continue in the foothills to St. Anne Lake and possibly to the southeast corner of the surveyed area. Rocks east of St. Anne Lake were considered by Chapin (1918) as of Early Jurassic age and by Moffitt (1938a) as of Carboniferous age. The numerous plutons known to be present in the northern Chugach Mountains are not sufficiently well mapped to permit correlation with the observed magnetic anomalies. However, some of the plutons are associated with magnetic highs.

High gravity values were recorded throughout the area occupied by the Chugach Mountains anomalies. The gravity contours form an elongate high that extends along the north side of the mountains and approximately coincides with the outcrops of Lower Jurassic volcanic rocks. Bouguer anomalies associated with these outcrops range from −15 to −35 mgal, or approximately 10 to 20 mgal higher than those in the Tyone Creek area where the same formation crops out. Part of the difference probably represents the regional gravity gradient across the Copper River Basin, and part may represent changes in the lithology of underlying rocks.

Low-gradient east-trending magnetic contours observed in the southeastern Copper River Basin just north of the Chugach Mountains anomalies indicate that if the magnetic rocks producing the northern Chugach Mountains anomalies continue northward under the sediments of the southeastern Copper River Basin, they are deeply buried.

TWIN LAKES ANOMALY

An irregular faulted anticline, in places exposing Lower Jurassic volcanic rocks along its axis and everywhere having Cretaceous marine sedimentary rocks on its flanks, is about 1 mile south of Twin Lakes in the southwestern corner of the surveyed area (pl. 23). The contrast between the magnetic susceptibility of the volcanic rocks and the essentially nonmagnetic sedimentary rocks produces the sharp Twin Lakes magnetic anomaly along the crest of the structure. The anomaly and the faulted anticline have a northeasterly trend, and the anomaly continues into the Copper River Basin a few miles beyond the northermost outcrops. Gravity data do not indicate any anomaly in the Twin Lakes area, but the station spacing is large, and a local anomaly might be masked by regional gradients.

AREAS WHERE LOWER JURASSIC VOLCANIC ROCKS ARE BURIED BY NONMAGNETIC ROCKS

The dashed lines shown on plate 23 approximately separate areas where magnetic rocks are at or near the surface from areas where magnetic rocks occur at greater depths. These lines, therefore, represent "lines of zero depth." They mark the south edge of the Tyone Creek anomalies and the north side of the Chugach Mountains anomalies. In most places the lines of zero depth also approximately coincide with the center of a group of closely spaced gravity contours and thus indicate a fairly abrupt change from dense to less dense rocks. The magnetic pattern between the dashed lines of zero depth and west of the dot-dash line at about long 146°15′ W. is also interpreted to have been produced by the Lower Jurassic volcanic rocks. However, the magnetic rocks in this area are farther from the plane of magnetic observation than in the Tyone Creek area, the Horn Mountains, or the northern Chugach Mountains, as evidenced by the less steep gradients and smaller amplitudes of the anomalies. The line of zero depth southeast of the Tyone Creek anomalies possibly represents a fault or homocline that may have placed the volcanic rocks at greater depths to the east and southeast.

It can be noted from an inspection of plate 23 that the magnetic pattern between the lines of zero depth shows in many places a northeasterly lineation that is approximately parallel to the trend of faults and fault blocks in the Nelchina area, which lies immediately west of the southwestern part of the Copper River Basin. This suggests that the structure of the southwestern Copper River Basin includes features similar to those of the Nelchina area. The anomalies in the southwestern Copper River Basin may be produced by magnetic rock masses at shallow or intermediate depths and may delineate fault blocks or faulted anticlines such as those that occur at Sheep Mountain or the Horn Mountains in the Nelchina area. The magnetic field observed over the east end of the Horn Mountains fault block, for example, differs from the magnetic field to the north and to the south, where magnetic rocks are more deeply buried. The areas of lowest magnetic gradient and amplitude in the southwestern Copper River Basin may indicate areas of thicker sediments between positive structures.

Lower Jurassic volcanic rocks crop out in the Tyone Creek and Horn Mountains areas and are also present in the intervening area under a cover of Jurassic and Cretaceous marine sedimentary rocks. The marine rocks rest unconformably on the Lower Jurassic volcanic rocks and dip to the south and southeast from the area of the Tyone Creek anomalies to a structural low near the Little Nelchina River, where geologic data indicate that the volcanic rocks are overlain by about 4,500 to 6,000 feet of sedimentary rocks. The increase in thickness of the marine sedimentary rocks from the Tyone

Creek anomaly area to the vicinity of the Little Nelchina River is also indicated by an increase in depths calculated from anomalies thought to be produced by the underlying volcanic rocks. The sedimentary rocks are about 4,000 to 5,000 feet thick at the fault bounding the Horn Mountains block on the north. South of this fault the Lower Jurassic volcanic rocks are at or near the surface.

The gravity is generally lower in the areas where sedimentary rocks cover the Lower Jurassic volcanic rocks. A gravity profile between the outcrops at Tyone Creek and the Horn Mountains would indicate a broad gravity low that reaches a minimum between the Little Nelchina River and upper Tyone Creek, which corresponds to the structural low indicated by geologic mapping. The Bouguer anomalies in the center of this line are approximately −55 mgal, or about 15 to 20 mgal below the values associated with the outcrops of Jurassic volcanic rocks. If these volcanic rocks and the associated or underlying Mesozoic sedimentary rocks continue with approximately constant thickness but increased depth between their two outcrops, the gravity anomaly would be caused by the cover of overlying sedimentary rocks and the deepening of the underlying basement rocks. Table 1 indicates that the density contrast between the Paleozoic basement rocks and the late Mesozoic sedimentary rocks is about 0.25 to 0.30 g per cm.^{3} Calculations based on this density contrast and the 15-20-mgal gravity anomaly suggest that the upper Mesozoic sedimentary rocks are 4,500 to 6,000 feet thick north of the Little Nelchina River. This thickness agrees closely with that inferred from geologic mapping.

The gravity low deepens and widens toward the center of the Copper River Basin and reaches a maximum near Old Man Lake. Thus, a broader and thicker sedimentary cover is probably present in the central part of the Basin. The magnetic patterns in this area resemble those in the Tyone Creek and Nelchina areas, but the anomalies are smoother and have lower amplitudes. The Lower Jurassic volcanic rocks and the structures they form may thus extend as far east as the dot-dash line on plate 23, or well beyond the lowest and widest part of the gravity low. The overlying sedimentary cover is discussed in the section, "Areas of thick sedimentary rocks."

Smooth and widely spaced magnetic contours over outcrops of Late Mesozoic sedimentary rocks suggest another thick sedimentary prism south of the Horn Mountains fault block and northwest of the Northern Chugach and Twin Lakes anomalies. However, there is no decrease in gravity along the south side of the Horn Mountains block and no indication of low gravity values in the area occupied by this suggested sedimentary prism. This absence of gravitational expression is not easily explained. It may suggest that the Horn Mountains fault block is not associated with a similar displacement of the Paleozoic basement rocks or that the Matanuska rocks south of the Horn Mountains have higher densities.

ANOMALIES IN THE SOUTHEASTERN PART OF THE SURVEYED AREA

Geophysical patterns in the eastern part of the southern Copper River Basin are probably caused by a greater variety of rock types. The Northern Chugach Mountains magnetic pattern extends to the southeast corner of the surveyed area, but the volcanic rocks causing the anomalies on the east end of the belt may be older than the Lower Jurassic volcanic rocks that crop out at its west end. North and south of this belt of Northern Chugach anomalies are the geophysical features described below.

CRANBERRY PEAK PATTERN

The Cranberry Peak pattern, along the south border of the surveyed area (pl. 23), is characterized by low magnetic gradients. These gradients are believed to be produced by the metamorphosed sedimentary rocks of Carboniferous and older (?) ages that are reported just north of Klutina Lake in the vicinity of Cranberry Peak. Most of the area mapped as being underlain by metasedimentary rock is characterized by low magnetic gradients, except in the extreme northeastern part. The approximate 2,000-gamma anomaly northeast of Mount Carter cannot be attributed to the metasedimentary rocks mapped there and suggests that this area is underlain at shallow depth by rocks similar to those that produce the northern Chugach Mountains magnetic anomalies.

Gravity decreases southward in the area occupied by the Cranberry Peak magnetic pattern, and Bouguer-anomaly values of −35 to −42 mgal occur along the north shore of Klutina Lake. This decrease in gravity toward the center of the Chugach Mountains may be caused either by isostatic effects or by an increasing thickness of Paleozoic sedimentary rocks that may be lighter than the volcanic rocks to the north.

DURHAM CREEK ANOMALY

The magnetic anomaly in the southcentral part of the Copper River Basin near Durham Creek, several miles north of the Chugach Mountains, has a maximum amplitude of about 125 gammas at its south end. This high yields a depth estimate of 2,000 feet to 3,000 feet to the upper surface of the mass causing the disturbance. Magnetic rocks causing this high apparently continue northward at an indeterminable depth about 5 miles north of the Glenn Highway, as evidenced by the flexure in the east-west trending magnetic contours. This area is approximately enclosed by the dotted line on plate 23.

The gravity profile along the Glenn Highway shows a positive anomaly of approximately 5 to 10 mgal associated with the Durham Creek magnetic anomaly, and the contour map suggests that the trend of the gravity anomaly may be more nearly northeastward rather than north-northeastward as indicated by the magnetic contours. However, the gravity stations north and south of the highway are very widely spaced, and the gravity contours cannot be drawn accurately. The Durham Creek gravity anomaly also seems to be considerably wider than the magnetic anomaly.

The Durham Creek anomaly is caused by a dense and magnetic rock mass that is not deeply buried. The rock is most likely igneous, and the low-amplitude anomaly may have been produced by a local steep-sided structural high on a magnetic basement surface or may indicate an intrusive body. A few other magnetic anomalies with north-south trends but with much smaller areas and low amplitudes occur to the east and west of the Durham Creek anomaly. These smaller magnetic anomalies are not associated with gravity anomalies.

MOUNT DRUM PATTERN

The Mount Drum pattern consists of a fanlike group of magnetic anomalies that project from the east edge of the surveyed area (pl. 24). The magnetic pattern is interpreted to be produced by andesitic lavas from the now extinct and dissected Mount Drum volcanic cone, the westernmost of the group of volcanoes that forms the Wrangell Mountains. This interpretation is based on the proximity of the magnetic pattern to Mount Drum, its coincidence with the topographic apron of Mount Drum, and its semicircular outline concentric to the mountain.

Anomalies within the Mount Drum pattern are considered unsuitable for quantitative depth analysis. However, the steep magnetic gradients in the center of the pattern near the edge of the surveyed area suggest that the lavas there are at or near ground surface. Magnetic gradients diminish toward the semicircular rim of the pattern, indicating that the lavas become thinner and more deeply buried there, perhaps to a depth of more than 500 feet near the rim.

The gravity decreases toward the Wrangell Mountains, where low Bouguer anomalies are caused by isostatic effects. A single station with a Bouguer anomaly of −94 mgal was observed near the center of the range in the valley of the upper Dadina River southeast of Mount Drum and east of the mapped area. A few

stations along the flanks of Mount Drum suggest that the gravity decreases from all directions toward the center of the mountain. Two areas of low gravity, the Glennallen and Gakona lows, extend west and northwest from the mountain toward the central part of the mapped area. Both these gravity lows extend considerably beyond the Mount Drum magnetic pattern. The intervening magnetic high and the gravity high associated with the West Fork feature also trend toward the center of the Wrangell Mountains. All the gravity gradients associated with these features are small and indicate either deep or gently sloping structures. The general trend of these Copper River Basin gravity anomalies toward the center of the Wrangell Mountains suggests that structures within the basin probably extend into the mountain ranges, where they are buried by the Cenozoic lavas.

AREAS OF THICK SEDIMENTARY ROCKS

Between the Mount Drum pattern and the Northern Chugach Mountains anomalies is a broad belt of low-gradient low-amplitude magnetic anomalies in which the Bouguer gravity anomalies range from −55 to −80 mgal. This belt of low-gradient anomalies trends southeast through Copper Center in an area where magnetic rocks are deeply buried and where there may be a great thickness of sedimentary rocks. However, the magnetic and gravity data do not preclude the occurrence of nonmagnetic crystalline rocks at shallow depths in this corner of the mapped area. Indeed, crystalline (metamorphosed Carboniferous sedimentary rocks) crop out in areas of rather low magnetic gradients and low gravity along the Edgerton Highway. However, lower magnetic gradients and lower gravity are observed immediately north of this area in a belt of very low magnetic gradients that trends through Copper Center. Upper Mesozoic sedimentary rocks which crop out on the southwest flank of the Wrangell Mountains may extend under this area and produce the very low gradients found there. However, these Mesozoic sediments are underlain in places by nonmagnetic basement rocks that might not be revealed by magnetic or gravity surveys.

ANOMALIES IN THE CENTRAL PART OF THE SURVEYED AREA

Previous sections of this paper have shown that many geophysical anomalies on the margins of the Copper River Basin can be related to geologic structures and lithologies that are already known or inferred from geologic mapping. Some anomalies extend into the central part of the basin and provide clues as to the rock types and structures that underlie the Quaternary sediment and alluvium. In the central part of the basin or the south-central part of the magnetic map there are also broad areas where low-gradient, or "flat," magnetic patterns suggest significant thicknesses of sedimentary rocks. However, such low-gradient magnetic patterns can also be produced by near-surface nonmagnetic crystalline rocks. Furthermore, igneous rocks (some lavas, for example) within a sedimentary section may produce magnetic anomalies sufficiently intense to mask anomalies produced by magnetic rocks beneath the sedimentary section, so that only the thickness of the sedimentary rocks above the higher igneous rocks can be estimated from the magnetic data. Additional information, geological or geophysical, is often necessary to help resolve these ambiguities.

Low Bouguer gravity anomalies, especially those that coincide with areas of low magnetic gradients, also suggest thick sedimentary sections and occur at three places in the Copper River Basin. These gravity lows and one pronounced magnetic feature are discussed below.

COPPER RIVER BASIN MAGNETIC ANOMALY

Immediately north of the Glenn Highway is a very broad east-trending magnetic anomaly that has an amplitude of approximately 300 to 400 gammas (pl. 23). Its character can be seen in figure 49, which shows north-south magnetic profiles $C-C'$, $D-D'$, and $E-E'$ across the surveyed area (pl. 23). The axis of the anomaly is approximately along lat 62°15′ N. and follows the projected trend of the Matanuska geosyncline but lies north of the deepest part on what may be tectonically the more stable side of the geosyncline. The large amplitude and low gradient of the Copper River Basin anomaly indicate that it is produced by a magnetic block (possibly a plutonic rock mass) whose upper surface may lie at a depth of as much as 10 miles. Similar magnetic anomalies over geosynclinal belts have been observed over Cook Inlet (Grantz, Zietz, and Andreasen, 1960) and over the Great Valley of California (Grantz and Zietz, 1960).

Gravity lows occupy much of the area along the axis of the Copper River Basin magnetic anomaly, but these lows are readily explained by rocks at shallower depths than those that cause the magnetic anomaly. Available data do not suggest a correlation between any gravity anomaly and the Copper River Basin magnetic anomaly. However, the low gravity values suggest that the magnetic anomaly may have a different origin from that of the magnetic anomaly in the Great Valley of California, where high gravity values have been measured.

OLD MAN LAKE GRAVITY ANOMALY

The most conspicuous feature of the gravity map is the broad low centered around Old Man Lake, where the Bouguer gravity anomalies are less than −80 mgal. Part of the area covered by this low is also an area where the magnetic gradients are low, and the coincidence of the two features suggests that this is the part of the Copper River Basin where the nonmagnetic rocks may be thickest. The Old Man Lake low lies along the axis of the Matanuska geosyncline and is in part a broadening and deepening of the gravity low between the Tyone Creek and Horn Mountains magnetic anomalies in the western part of the surveyed area. However, the continuity of the gravity anomaly does not imply lithologic continuity for the rocks which may explain it. The difference between the gravity over the sedimentary rocks north of the Horn Mountains and the gravity over the outcrops of Jurassic volcanic rocks is 15 to 20 mgal, and a reasonable thickness of the overlying upper Jurassic and Cretaceous sedimentary rocks can be calculated by using a density contrast of 0.25 to 0.30 g per cm³, the average difference between measured densities of Paleozoic metamorphosed rocks and upper Mesozoic sedimentary rocks. At Old Man Lake the gravity anomaly relative to the outcrops of Lower Jurassic volcanic rocks is 40 to 50 mgls, and if the same assumptions apply (see the discussions on p. 139), the thickness of overlying upper Mesozoic rocks is 10,000 to 15,000 feet.

It is assumed that the whole gravity anomaly is caused by thickening of the upper Mesozoic sedimentary rocks and depression of the Paleozoic basement rocks and that the lower Mesozoic and upper Carboniferous sedimentary and volcanic rocks underlie the basin in a layer of nearly uniform thickness and density. However, part of the anomaly is probably caused by an increase in thickness of Talkeetna and pre-Talkeetna rocks, so the overlying upper Mesozoic sedimentary rocks are probably thinner than 10,000 to 15,000 feet. Density differences are also poorly known and are based largely on samples from outcrops along the margins of the basin. Geologic data suggests that the densities within the basin may be lower and that facies changes eastward from the Nelchina area may include a change from volcanic to less dense sedimentary rock types. Lower density contrasts within the basin would increase the calculated values of sedimentary thicknesses, and higher contrasts would decrease them.

The gravity gradients forming the Old Man Lake low are quite gentle (ranging from 1 to 4 mgal per mi), and the anomaly could be partly explained or influenced by deeply buried density contrasts. Either isostatic effects or the deeply buried rock mass suggested by the

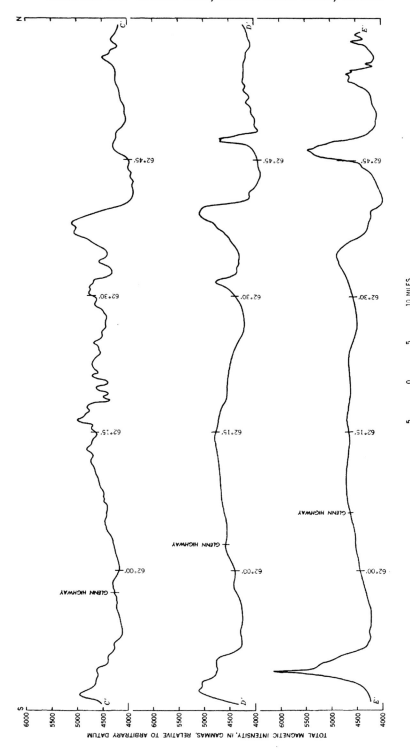

FIGURE 49.—North-south aeromagnetic profiles C-C', D-D', and E-E' across the Copper River Basin area, Alaska

Copper River Basin magnetic anomaly could influence the magnitude of the anomaly and the depths calculated from it. The largest gravity gradients were measured along the northwest shore of Tazlina Lake and along the west shore of Susitna Lake. These gradients are assumed to represent steeply dipping faults or contacts between the Jurassic volcanic rocks and the upper Mesozoic (and possibly Tertiary) sedimentary rocks.

The magnetic lineations over much of the area occupied by the Old Man Lake gravity anomaly reflect structural patterns similar to those of the Nelchina area, and the Lower Jurassic volcanic rocks probably extend at depth as far east as the dot-dash line on plate 23. The observed magnetic gradients may be caused by susceptibility contrasts or by fault blocks or faulted anticlines within the Lower Jurassic rocks. Estimates of the depth to the magnetic rock masses can be estimated by the Vacquier method (Vacquier and others, 1951). Although most magnetic anomalies in the vicinity of Old Man Lake are not entirely satisfactory for depth analysis, gradients of some nearby anomalies indicate that the magnetic rock masses are from 2,000 to 5,000 feet below the land surface. Bouguer anomalies near these magnetic anomalies range from −45 to −65 mgal and suggest that the overlying sedimentary section may be thicker than is indicated by the magnetic anomalies. However, if the inferred volcanic rocks thin significantly to the east, depth estimates based on the anomalies may be too shallow; hence, the anomaly producing rocks may be buried at depths closer to those suggested by the gravity data.

If the magnetic character of the Lower Jurassic volcanic rocks in the area of the Old Man Lake anomaly is essentially the same as in the areas of outcrop, and if the rocks are at least a few thousand feet thick, it is possible to determine the approximate depth of the top of the magnetic blocks through application of the method of upward continuation used by Henderson and Zietz (1949). A magnetic profile along a flight line over exposed Lower Jurassic volcanic rocks can be projected vertically upward until it resembles an observed north-south profile over the area interpreted to be underlain by the same rocks at depth. As the magnetic profile is continued upward, the gradients and amplitudes decrease. Profile A–A' (pl. 23; fig. 50) was continued upward to several levels of observation, and the projected profiles were then compared with profile B–B' (pl. 23; fig. 50). Profiles A–A' and B–B' were observed at a flight elevation of 4,000 feet. When A–A' was continued upward to elevations of 9,000 feet and 10,000 feet, it compared favorably with profile B–B'. Magnetic profile A–A', its upward continuations, and B–B' are shown in figure 50, where it can

be seen that profile A–A' would closely resemble B–B' if A–A' had been flown at an elevation of 9,000 or 10,000 feet. As the Lower Jurassic rocks are at or near the ground surface in the vicinity of A–A', they could very likely be present in the vicinity of B–B' at a depth equivalent to the distance of upward continuation—namely 5,000 to 6,000 feet.

Bouguer anomalies along profile B–B' range from −27 mgal at the north end to −65 mgal at the south end and indicate a significant variation of sediment thickness along the profile. The anomaly at the center of the profile is about −53 mgal, which would yield a depth estimate of about 5,000 feet by the analysis used successfully at the west side of the basin. Thus, depth estimates from gravity data and from upward continuation of magnetic data are approximately the same, but both estimates should probably be considered maximal because of the assumptions inherent in the analyses. Furthermore, agreement occurs near the margin of the gravity low, and agreement between magnetic and gravity depth estimates is not satisfactory at places closer to the center of the gravity low.

GLENNALLEN AND GAKONA GRAVITY LOWS

Two other gravity lows lie east of the Old Man Lake low and merge with the gravity low associated with the Wrangell Mountains. One of these gravity lows is centered south of the town of Glennallen; and the second is centered northwest of Gakona. In both areas magnetic gradients are low, but the areas of lowest magnetic gradient do not coincide with the areas of lowest gravity. Minimum gravity values occur close to the Wrangell Mountains in the area of the Mount Drum magnetic pattern. The two areas of lowest magnetic gradients are south of Crosswind Lake and between Gulkana and Ewan Lake. Bouguer gravity anomalies lower than −55 mgal and low magnetic gradients cover almost the whole area between the Old Man Lake, Glennallen, and Gakona gravity anomalies. On the west edge of the Copper River Basin, such low Bouguer anomalies and magnetic gradients are typical of the Old Man Lake area and suggest that the overlying sedimentary rocks are at least 5,000 feet thick and probably 10,000 to 15,000 feet thick; a similar thickness may occur in the eastern part of the basin. However, the outcrops of metamorphosed Carboniferous sedimentary rocks along the Edgerton Highway in the southeast corner of the area show that low susceptibility, and possibly low-density, rocks may underlie much of the southeast corner of the Copper River Basin, where both Bouguer gravity anomalies and magnetic gradients are low.

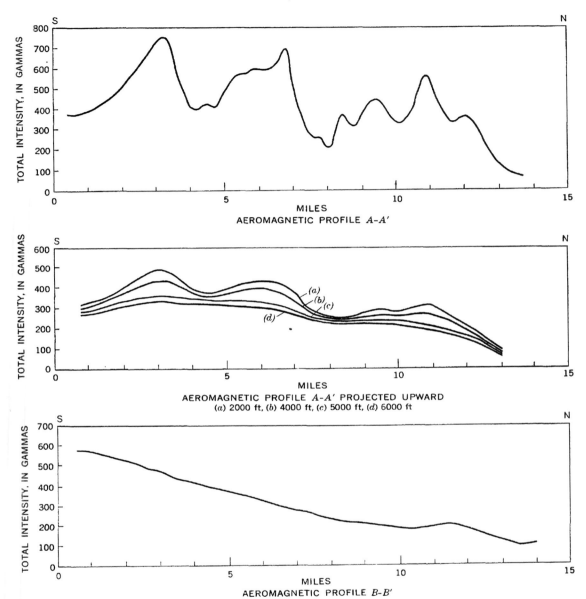

FIGURE 50.—Upward continuation of the magnetic field observed over outcrops of Lower Jurassic volcanic rocks (A-A', pl. 23) compared with an observed magnetic profile (B-B', pl. 23) where these rocks are at depth.

Gravity contours between the three main gravity lows are based primarily on profiles along the Glenn and Richardson Highways. There are only a few gravity stations in the broad area between Glennallen, Crosswind Lake, and Ewan Lake, and the elevations of these few stations were obtained by altimetry. Gravity contours in this area on plate 24 are dashed because of the scarcity of gravity stations and the uncertainty of the elevation measurements. Hence, the relationship between the three gravity lows may be correspondingly uncertain.

The Glennallen gravity low is along the projection of the belt of upper Mesozoic sedimentary rocks along the south side of the Wrangell Mountains and occurs over an area of very low magnetic gradients that extends through Copper Center and Glennallen. One of the areas of lowest magnetic gradients lies along this same projection south and southeast of Crosswind Lake. If the upper Mesozoic rocks mapped on the south side of the Wrangell Mountains extend northwestward into the Copper River Basin, they may be thickest in the very low magnetic gradient area that extends through Copper Center and Glennallen and in the area south and southeast of Crosswind Lake.

Lower Jurassic sedimentary rocks that occur in the Chitina Valley represent a facies change from the predominantly volcanic rocks of the same age in the Nelchina area. The sedimentary facies probably extends underneath the area occupied by the Glennallen and Gakona gravity lows in the eastern part of the Copper River Basin. The dot-dash line on plate 23 approximates the eastern limit of the area of Lower Jurassic rocks containing a significant proportion of lava flows and tuffs. Also, the Upper Triassic and Carboniferous sedimentary rocks of the Chitina Valley probably extend under the southeast Copper River Basin. These sedimentary rocks would not be indicated by the magnetic data, but they may contribute to the gravity anomaly; so thickness calculations from the gravity data have not been attempted. A final unknown factor might be the presence of a significant thickness of low-density Tertiary sedimentary rocks, especially in the northern part of the Copper River Basin.

CONCLUSIONS

The geophysical data collected from approximately 6,000 square miles in the Copper River Basin provide considerable information of geologic interest. In general, the magnetic and gravity patterns can be correlated with the regional east-trending geologic grain and topographic features. Areas where volcanic rocks crop out are well defined by the observed magnetic patterns, and these volcanic rocks are clearly indicated to be present elsewhere under a cover of younger nonmagnetic rocks.

Approximately the northern third of the surveyed area is characterized by bands of steep-gradient east-trending magnetic highs and lows produced by alternate bands of magnetic and nonmagnetic rocks at or near the land surface. The lack of detailed geologic mapping in this area precludes positive correlation with rock units, but the observed magnetic patterns should be of considerable help in future geologic mapping.

Magnetic anomalies observed in the west-central part of the surveyed area are produced by the Lower Jurassic volcanic rocks of the Talkeetna Formation. The magnetic pattern over most of the southwestern part of

the surveyed area is interpreted as produced by the Lower Jurassic volcanic rocks generally present under the sedimentary rocks at depths ranging from about 2,000 to 5,000 feet but even deeper if the volcanic rocks are thin.

The steep-gradient high-amplitude magnetic anomalies that are elongated in an easterly direction over the northern Chugach Mountains are interpreted as produced by volcanic rocks with associated intrusive rocks. Metamorphosed sedimentary rocks of Carboniferous and older(?) ages reported in the Cranberry Peak area of the northern Chugach Mountains are characterized by low magnetic gradients.

The areal extent of the lavas of the Wrangell Mountains is well outlined by their magnetic pattern. They deepen and probably thin to the west and, in the vicinity of Glennallen, may be covered by 500 feet or more of glacial deposits.

Two broad areas having low-gradient magnetic intensity occur in the Copper River Basin. One area occupies the southwestern part of the surveyed area; the other approximately parallels the course of the Copper River. Within the area that parallels the Copper River are three zones of very low gradient magnetic intensity: (1) the Copper Center vicinity, (2) the area immediately south of Crosswind Lake, and (3) the area between Gulkana and Ewan Lake.

Three negative gravity anomalies, which may indicate areas where sedimentary rocks are thick, correlate with areas of low magnetic gradients: (1) a broad east-trending gravity low in the southwest Copper River Basin centered approximately at Old Man Lake, (2) a gravity low in the vicinity of Glennallen, and (3) a gravity low north and west of Gulkana.

REFERENCES CITED

Andreasen, G. E., Dempsey, W. J., Henderson, J. R., and Gilbert, F. P., 1958, Aeromagnetic map of the Copper River Basin, Alaska: U.S. Geol. Survey Geophys. Inv. Map GP–156.

Chapin, Theodore, 1918, The Nelchina-Susitna region, Alaska: U.S. Geol. Survey Bull. 668, 67 p.

Grantz, Arthur, 1953, Preliminary report on the geology of the Nelchina area, Alaska: U.S. Geol. Survey open-file report.

———— 1960, Generalized geologic map of the Nelchina area, Alaska, showing igneous rocks and larger basalts: U.S. Geol. Survey Misc. Geol. Inv. Map I–312.

Grantz, Arthur, Zietz, Isidore, and Andreasen, G. E., 1960, An aeromagnetic reconnaissance of the Cook Inlet area, Alaska: U.S. Geol. Survey open-file report, 66 p.

Grantz, Arthur, and Zietz, Isidore, 1960, Possible significance of broad magnetic highs over belts of moderately deformed sedimentary rocks in Alaska and California: U.S. Geol. Survey Prof. Paper 400–B, p. B342–B347.

Henderson, R. G., and Zietz, Isidore, 1949, The upward continuation of anomalies in total intensity fields: Geophysics, v. 14, no. 4, p. 517–534.

Hyslop, R. C., 1945, A field method for determining the magnetic susceptibiilty of rocks: Am. Inst. Mining Metall. Engineers Trans., v. 164, p. 242–246.

Mendenhall, W. C., 1905, Geology of the Central Copper River Region, Alaska: U.S. Geol. Survey Prof. Paper 41, 133 p.

Moffit, F. H., 1912, Headwater regions of Gulkana and Susitna River, Alaska: U.S. Geol. Survey Bull. 498, 82 p.

——— 1938a, Geology of the Chitina Valley and adjacent area, Alaska,: U.S. Geol. Survey Bull. 894, 137 p.

——— 1938b, Geology of the Slana-Tok district, Alaska: U.S. Geol. Survey Bull. 904, 54 p.

——— 1954, Geology of the eastern part of the Alaska Range and adjacent area: U.S. Geol. Survey Bull. 989–D, p. 63–218.

Payne, T. G., 1955, Mesozoic and Cenozoic tectonic elements cf Alaska: U.S. Geol. Survey Misc. Geol. Inv. Map. I–84.

Thiel, Edward, Bonini, W. E., Ostenson, N. A., and Woollard, G. P., 1958, Gravity measurements in Alaska: Woods Hole Oceanographic Institution Tech. Reports, Ref. 58–54, 104 p.

Vacquier, Victor, Steenland, N. C., Henderson, R. G., and Zietz, Isidore, 1951, Interpretation of aeromagnetic maps: Geol. Soc. America Mem. 47, 151 p.

Vestine, E. H., Laporte, L., Lange, I., Cooper, C., and Hendrix, W. C., 1947, Description of the earth's main magnetic field and its secular change, 1905–1945: Carnegie Inst. Washington, Dept. Terrestrial Magnetism Pub. 578, p. 466.

Wahrhaftig, Clyde, 1960, Physiographic provinces of Alaska: U.S. Geol. Survey open-file report, 78 p.

CPSIA information can be obtained at www.ICGtesting.com
Printed in the USA
BVOW06s2308141013

333758BV00008B/256/P